Copyright © 2020 by Desiree Aidoo

Jai Publishing
WRITE. RELEASE. HEAL.

All rights reserved. No part of this publication may be reproduced, distributed, or transmitted in any form or by any means, including photocopying, recording, or other electronic or mechanical methods, without the prior written permission of the publisher, except in the case of brief quotations embodied in critical reviews and certain other noncommercial uses permitted by copyright law.

For permission requests, write to the publisher, addressed "Attention: Permissions Coordinator," at the address below.

Jai Publishing House Incorporated
1230 Peachtree Street NE, 19th Floor
Atlanta, Georgia 30309
www.jaipublishing.com

DISCLAIMER

Images used in this cookbook are stock images purchased by the publishing company. In regard to food allergies, some of these recipes contain peanuts, tree nuts, soy, milk, eggs and wheat. None of the recipes or advice given in this cookbook intend to diagnose, treat, cure or prevent any disease. Content should not be considered a substitute for professional medical expertise or treatment. Neither the author or publisher will be held liable for any adverse effect that may result from the use or application of the information contained in this cookbook. Use of brand names does not imply approval or endorsement from the brand.

Printed in the United States of America
ISBN-13: 978-1-7352082-5-1

Baking With Someone Special

How one little girl with Autism inspired a baking business

Desiree Aidoo & Kyla Renee Wilson

In Loving Memory of my beautiful sister

Silvia G. Pierce

Table of Contents

Apple Cake 9

Apple Pie 11

Banana Bread 13

Blueberry And Lemon Scones 15

Chocolate Cake 17

Cream Cheese Frosting 19

Hazelnut Spread Pecan Bars 21

Hummingbird Cake 23

Lemon Bars 25

Lemon Pound Cake 27

Oatmeal Raisin Cookies 29

PB & J Thumb Print Cookies 31

Peach Pie 33

Pumpkin Bread 35

Rasberry Oatmeal Bars 37

Red Velvet Sugar Cookies 39

Salted Caramel Brownie 41

Smores Cookies 43

Spice Cake 45

Spice Muffin 47

Strawberry Buns 49

Strawberry Cake 51

Vanilla Cake 53

Vanilla Confetti Cupcakes 55

White chocolate chip cookies 57

Meet Kyla 58

Introduction

Dear Friend,

Both Kyla and I are super excited to share our recipes with you that has helped foster a healthy relationship between us. We share a love of baking, and used that shared love to build a business doing what I love every single day! Plus, I get to spend more time with my adorable granddaughter, Kyla, my inspiration for it all.

Sometimes, you just have to get a little dirty, have fun, enjoy life, enjoy time with family, and let your hair down. Trust me, your mental health will thank you. :-)

We hope that being in the kitchen with your unique and gifted child(ren), baking up these sugary goodness, will strengthen a bond of love, grace, and compassion for family and relationships.

Now get in that kitchen and BAKE! And, don't forget the most important ingredient, you can't do anything without it: FUN! :-)

Happy baking,

Apple Cake Storyline

In our neighborhood, there's a park with an apple tree in it. When Kyla was younger, we'd visit this park. Kyla absolutely loves swinging on the swings. In addition to playing, Kyla would pick apples and we'd go home and bake apple turnovers, apple pie and apple cake. She was very helpful and really enjoyed washing the apples as well as helping to add the sugar and spices. Her younger brother is very fond of apples, too. Kyla would save some for him. This cake is one of our favorites!

Apple Cake

2 ½ cups of all purpose flour
2 ½ teaspoons of baking powder
¼ teaspoon of salt
1 teaspoon of cinnamon
3 eggs
1 ½ stick of softened unsalted butter
2 tablespoons of vanilla extract
2 tablespoons of sour cream
½ of a 21 ounce can of pie filling apples
1 ¼ cups of milk
1 ½ cups of granulated sugar
1 3.9 oz. box of instant vanilla pudding

1. In a bowl, mix the flour, baking powder, salt, vanilla pudding, and cinnamon until well combined.
2. In a separate bowl. Cut your apple slices issn half.
3. Using a mixer. Cream together the butter and sugar until fluffy. And your eggs one at a time. Making sure each one is well blended before adding the next.
4. Slowly begin to add your flour mixture, alternating with your milk.
5. Make sure to occasionally scrape down the sides of your bowl.
6. Lastly add your sour cream and mix until just blended.
7. Using a mixing spoon, fold in your apples and pour into two 8-inch baking pans greased or sprayed with cooking spray.
8. Bake up to 45 minutes or until an inserted toothpick comes out clean.
9. Cool in pans for 5 minutes, then remove and place on a cooling rack.

Apple Pie

1 package of pie crust that comes (two in a pack)
1 cup granulated sugar
1 cup of water
1 tbsp lemon juice
¼ cup cornstarch
1 tsp vanilla extract
¼ tsp cinnamon powder
5 cups frozen or fresh peeled Granny Smith apples
Preheat oven to 375 degrees F

1. In a large saucepan, combine the lemon juice, sugar, water and cornstarch and simmer on medium heat until the sauce thickens. Stir often to prevent lumps. Remove from heat. Add the cinnamon, vanilla extract and apples. Mix thoroughly. Let the mixture cool completely.
2. Prepare your crust by rolling one of the pie crust into a 9 inch pie dish. Pour your cooled pie filling into the dish. Unroll your other pie crust and loosely cover the pie.
3. Use your hands to pinch together and crimp the two pie crust edges. Use a knife to cut slits into the top off the pie crust. This allows steam to escape as the pie filling is heating up and the crust is baking.
4. Use foil paper to cover the edges of the pie to prevent burning. Bake at 375 degrees for 30-45 minutes or until the crust is golden brown.

Bon Appétit!

Banana Bread

2 cups all purpose flour
1 cup of sugar
1 teaspoon of salt
1 teaspoon of baking soda
1 teaspoon of baking powder
1 teaspoon of ground cinnamon
2 tablespoon of whole milk
2 large eggs
3 ripe bananas
1 stick of room temperature unsalted butter

1. Preheat oven to 325 degrees.
2. Butter and flour a 9 inch loaf pan and set aside. You can also use cooking spray instead of the butter and flour.
3. Cream sugar and butter in a large bowl until light and fluffy.
4. Add eggs one at a time, mixing each one well before adding the other one.
5. In another bowl, mash bananas with a fork. Mix in milk and cinnamon.
6. In another bowl, mix dry ingredients: flour, baking soda, baking powder, and salt.
7. Then mix the banana and creamed butter together. Add slowly in the dry ingredients until just combined.
8. Pour batter into your 9 inch loaf pan and bake anywhere from 1 hour to 1 hour and 10 minutes or until a toothpick inserted in the center comes out clean.
9. Let bread cool in the pan for 20 minutes. Remove and place on a flat surface to cool completely before cutting it.

Enjoy!!

Blueberry And Lemon Scones

2 cups all purpose flour
2 tsp baking powder
⅓ cup sugar
¾ tsp salt
¼ cup milk
10 tbsp frozen unsalted butter
¾ tsp lemon extract
2 tbsp lemon juice
1 eggs
6 oz, fresh or frozen blueberries

1. Preheat the oven to 400 degrees F and line a baking sheet with parchment paper.
2. In a large bowl, combine all of the dry ingredients and whisk together. Next, grate your frozen butter into the flour mixture. Mix together using a fork or hands.
3. In another bowl, mix all of the wet ingredients (including the eggs) and whisk together.
4. Create a well in the center of the dry ingredients and pour your wet ingredients into it, including the blueberries. Now take a fork and gently mix it together. (if your dough appears too dry, add an additional 1-2 tbsp of milk.)
5. For this next part, you have to flour your hands to prevent the dough from sticking. On a surface area, use your hands to turn dough onto your surface. You can shape the dough in a square and cut into triangles or break off pieces to form a round biscuit shape.
6. Place your scones on your prepared baking sheet and brush with egg wash (Recipe also included in this book).
7. It is important that you place your scones in the freezer for 15 minutes to refreeze your butter. Do this step before baking.
8. Bake for 20-25 minutes until golden brown. Once completely cooled, you can drizzle with the lemon glaze (recipe included in this book).

Chocolate Cake Storyline

Kyla's favorite of all time is chocolate. She inherited this chocolate trait from her mother, who is also very fond of chocolate. Her mom always kept milk chocolate candy bars in her purse, and would give Kyla chocolate. Kyla discovered her mom's hiding place at a very young age. And was often caught either searching through her mom's purse or enjoying the chocolate she'd found. Milk chocolate is the only chocolate bar she will eat. We tried other kinds, such as mint and dark chocolate. Kyla wants nothing to do with them. But she loves chocolate cake. She helps me make the chocolate frosting. She's usually laughing and smiling during the entire process..

Chocolate Cake

1 ¾ cups all purpose flour
¾ cup unsweetened cocoa powder
1 ½ tsp baking soda
1 ½ tsp baking powder
1 tsp salt
2 eggs
1 cup of whole milk
½ cup vegetable oil
2 tsp vanilla extract
1 cup boiling hot instant coffee

1. Preheat the oven to 350 degrees F.
2. Grease and flour two 8- or 9-inch baking pans or spray them with cooking spray.
3. In a large bowl, stir together the sugar, flour, cocoa, baking powder, baking soda, and salt.
4. Add the eggs, milk, vanilla, and oil. Mix for two minutes at medium speed.
5. Lastly, stir in the boiling hot coffee. Please note that this batter will be thin, it is perfectly OK. But don't let that confuse you. If you follow all the directions, you are on track.
6. Next, pour batter evenly into pans. Bake for 30-35 minutes or until an inserted toothpick comes out clean. Cool in pans for 10 minutes. Remove from pans and place on a wire rack to completely cool. Once cooled, frost with your favorite frosting and enjoy.

Cream Cheese Frosting

½ cup of vegetable shortening or softened butter
8 ounces of softened cream cheese
4 cups confectioners sugar
2 teaspoons vanilla extract

1. Beat butter and cream cheese together until well mixed.
2. Add vanilla, then add powdered sugar one cup at a time.
3. Beat until creamy.

Hazelnut Spread Pecan Bars

1 cup packed brown sugar
1 cup unsalted butter softened
1 tsp baking soda
2 ½ cups all purpose flour
1 3.4 oz of instant vanilla pudding
½ tsp salt
1 egg
1 tsp vanilla extract
1 can of sweetened condensed milk
½ cup of hazelnut spread
½ cup chopped pecans

1. Preheat the oven to 350 degrees F.
2. Spray a 13x9 inch baking pan with a lot of cooking spray.
3. In a bowl, mix together salt, baking soda, pudding mix, and flour.
4. In another bowl, using a stand or hand mixer, cream together butter and brown sugar until light and fluffy. Add your egg and vanilla to it and mix again. Next add your flour to the mixture and blend until it becomes a soft dough. Press half of the dough evenly into the bottom of your baking pan and bake for 15 minutes. Once baked, allow it to cool slightly.
5. Now in another small bowl, whisk together your hazelnut spread and condensed milk. Spread the mixture evenly over the cookie dough in your baking pan. Crumble the remaining dough evenly over the hazelnut spread with your hands. Top it off with the chopped pecans and place back in the oven. Bake for 30 minutes or until it has a beautiful deep golden brown color.
6. Cool completely before cutting into bar.

Bon Appétit!

Hummingbird Storyline

Hummingbird cake is a very rich tasting cake filled with a lot of different textures. Kyla's Autism makes this cake a big, "no can do" for her :). But the name reminds me of one her favorite loves – nature. She inherited this trait from her dad, who also loves the outdoors. One year, her mom grew a small vegetable garden in the backyard. Kyla was delighted! She loved digging in the garden, helping her mom prune weeds. And when the time was right, she helped pick tomatoes and kale. She's very fond of the outdoors. On one occasion, Kyla was in the kiddie pool accompanied by chipmunks. The chipmunks were swimming all around and she just sat there calmly in her own world. I thought her mom was going to pass out!

Hummingbird Cake

3 cups of all purpose flour
1 tsp salt
1 tsp cinnamon
1/2 tsp allspice
1 1/2 cup of vegetable oil
2 cups granulated sugar
3 eggs
2 ripe bananas (chopped in small cube pieces)
1 8oz can of crushed pineapple (drained)
2 tsp baking soda
2 tsp vanilla extract
2 cups chopped pecans
(place one cup of nuts aside for garnish)
⅓ cup sourcream

1. Preheat oven to 350 degrees
2. Combine flour, salt, baking soda, cinnamon, and allspice in a bowl. Whisk together.
3. In a separate bowl, combine sugar, eggs, vanilla extract, sour cream, oil, chopped banana, and pineapple. Once mixed, add half of the flour mixture to the wet ingredients. Slowly fold it in, until just combined.
4. Add the remaining flour mixture and pecans. Folding them in until just combined. Over mixing will make your cake texture tough when baked.
5. Once combined, separate batter into 3 greased (vegetable shortening) and floured 8-inch cake pans.
6. Bake for 25-30 minutes or until a toothpick comes out clean. Cool in pans for 10 minutes then turn onto a cooling rack until completely cooled.
7. I like to place a small napkin or towel over my cakes until completely cooled. Once cooled, you can build your cake by adding your frosting of choice between each layer. My go-to for this cake is cream cheese frosting (recipe in this book).

Lemon Bars

2 ¼ cups of all purpose flour
2 cups of granulated sugar
1 cup of cold butter, cut in small pieces
4 eggs
¾ cup of lemon juice

1. Preheat the oven to 350 degree F.
2. Grease and a 13x9 inch baking pan and line it with parchment paper.
3. Use a food processor, pastry cutter, or a fork to combine ½ cup of the sugar, 2 cups of the flour, and the cup of cold butter. Press into your baking pan.
4. Bake for 20 minutes until edges are starting to turn golden brown.
5. For the top layer: Whisk together the remaining sugar, flour, eggs, and lemon juice until sugar is dissolved. Let it sit for 10 minutes and whisk together again. Pour batter over the top of the crust and spread evenly.
6. Bake for 20-25 minutes or until the top is golden brown. When the custard appears to be set, cool completely. Then sprinkle powdered sugar over the top of the bar, cut and serve.

Bon Appétit!

Lemon Pound Cake

1 ½ cups granulated sugar
¾ cup butter unsalted butter softened
1 ¾ cups all purpose flour
1 8oz box of instant pudding mix
1 ¼ cups whole milk
⅓ cup of vegetable oil
4 eggs
2 tsp lemon extract
1 tsp salt
4 tsp baking powder
3 tbsp cornstarch

1. Preheat oven to 325 degree F.
2. Grease and flour (or spray with a cooking spray) a regular/standard sized bundt pan. Set it aside.
3. In a bowl, mix together all of the dry ingredients including pudding mix. A whisk will do just fine.
4. Next, cream together butter and sugar until light and fluffy (using a stand or hand mixer on medium speed). Then add eggs one at a time until well incorporated, then add lemon extract.
5. Next, combine milk and oil and whisk together. Start mixing the two by slowly adding the dry ingredients into the butter mixture. Alternating with the milk/oil mixture.   And end with the milk/oil.
6. Mix on medium speed for two minutes. Pour mixture into the prepared bundt pan and bake for 50-60 minutes or until an inserted toothpick comes out clean.
7. Let cool in a pan for 10 minutes. Then turn on to a cooling rack. Once cooled, frost with your favorite frosting or glaze.

Yum!

Oatmeal Raisin Cookies

2 cups all purpose flour
1 cup granulated sugar
1 cup brown sugar
2 eggs
1tsp baking powder
1 tsp salt
1 ½ cups unsalted butter
3 cups old fashioned rolled oats
1 ½ cups raisins
1 tsp vanilla extract
¼ tsp nutmeg
¾ tsp cinnamon

1. Preheat the oven to 375 degree F.
2. Line a baking sheet with parchment paper.
3. In a large bowl, mix all dry ingredients except the oats and raisins.
4. In another bowl, using a hand or stand mixer, cream together both sugars and butter until fluffy.
5. Then mix in the eggs, one at a time, and your vanilla. Mix well.
6. Add your oats and your raisins. Mix until just combined. Don't over mix.
7. Using a small ice cream scoop or a spoon, scoop mixture on to your baking sheet. Don't crown them, but space the cookie dough about 2 inches apart.
8. Bake for 12-14 minutes until golden around the edges.
9. Let cool for 5 minutes.

PB & J Thumb Print Cookies

2 eggs
1 cup all purpose flour
1 tsp baking powder
½ tsp salt
1 ½ cup chunky or creamy peanut butter divided
½ cup of softened peanut butter
1 ½ cups granulated sugar
½ cup brown sugar
1tsp vanilla extract
⅓ cup strawberry jelly

1. Preheat oven to 350 degrees F.
2. In a bowl, mix together all of your dry ingredients.
3. In another bowl, using a stand or hand mixer, mix together the eggs and peanut butter until smooth and creamy. Now add your eggs one at a time. And your vanilla until well mixed.
4. Stir in your flour mixture, until just combined.
5. Using a spoon or a small ice cream scoop, place 1 ½ in balls of cookie dough 2 inches apart on a baking sheet lined with parchment paper.
6. Use your thumb to place an indentation in each cookie.
7. And place 1 tsp of jelly in each middle of the cookie dough.
8. Bake 12-13 minutes until lightly golden in color.

Bon Appétit!

Peach Pie

1 package of pie crust (two in a pack)
1 cup granulated sugar
1 cup of water
1 tbsp lemon juice
¼ cup cornstarch
1 tsp vanilla extract
¼ tsp cinnamon powder
5 cups frozen or fresh peeled peaches

1. Preheat oven to 375 degrees F.
2. In a large saucepan, combine the lemon juice, sugar, water and cornstarch on medium heat until the sauce thickens. Stir often to prevent lumps.
3. Once sauce is thick enough for your taste, remove from heat. Add the cinnamon, vanilla extract and peaches and mix thoroughly. Let the mixture cool completely.
4. Prepare your crust by rolling one of the pie crust into a 9 inch pie dish. Pour your cooled pie filling into the dish. Unroll your other pie dish and loosely cover the pie. Use your hands to pinch together and crimp the two pie crust edges.
5. Use a knife to cut slits into the top off the pie crust. This allows steam to escape as the pie filling is heating up and the crust baking.
6. Use foil paper to cover the edges of the pie to prevent burning.
7. Bake at 375 degrees for 30-45 minutes or until the crust is golden brown.

Yummy Yum Yum!

Pumpkin Bread

3 ½ cups all purpose flour
2 tsp baking soda
1 tsp ground cinnamon
3 tsp pumpkin spice seasoning
1 ½ tsp salt
1 tsp vanilla extract
1 16oz can of packed pumpkin
1 cup vegetable oil
⅔ cup of water
4 eggs
3 cups granulated sugar

1. Preheat oven to 325 degree F.
2. Grease (or spray with cooking spray) two 8x4 loaf baking pans.
3. In a bowl, mix all dry ingredients.
4. In another bowl, whisk together all of the other ingredients including the canned pumpkin.
5. Mix in the flour mixture one cup at a time, until well mixed. Don't over mix the batter.
6. Pour batter evenly in the two baking pans and bake for 75-80 minutes or until a toothpick comes out clean. Cool in pans 10-15 minutes before removing to a drying rack to completely cool.

Bon Appétit!

Rasberry Oatmeal Bars

3 cups all purpose flour
1 tsp salt
1 tsp vanilla extract
3 cups of old fashioned rolled oats
1 ½ cups unsalted butter
2 cups packed brown sugar
1 tsp baking powder
1 18 oz jar of raspberry jam

1. Preheat oven to 350 degrees F.
2. Grease a 13x9 baking pan
3. Using a stand or hand mixer, cream together sugar and butter until creamy.
4. In another bowl, whisk together, flour, oats, salt, and baking powder.
5. Add to creamed butter and sugar. And add vanilla. Mix well.
6. Press ¾ of the mixture into your baking pan.
7. Spread the jam evenly over the oat mixture and crumble the rest on top.
8. Bake 40-45 minutes until golden brown and the jam is bubbling.
9. Allow to completely cool before cutting and Enjoy!

Red Velvet Sugar Cookies

3 cups all purpose flour

1 cup granulated sugar

1 cup unsalted butter

¼ cup unsweetened cocoa powder

¼ cup cornstarch

½ tsp salt

1 tsp red (no taste) gel food coloring (wilton has an excellent one)

2 tsp vanilla extract

1 large egg yolk

½ of a 8oz block of cream cheese

1. Preheat oven to 375 degree F.
2. Line a baking sheet with parchment paper.
3. In a bowl, combine flour, salt, cocoa, and cornstarch.
4. In a separate bowl, using a stand or hand mixer on medium-low speed, cream together cream cheese, sugar, and butter until smooth.
5. Next, add the food coloring, egg yolk, and vanilla extract. Mix on medium speed until well combined. Make sure to scrape down the sides of the bowl to mix it well.
6. Next, add your flour mixture. Mix on medium to low speed until it forms a ball of dough.
7. Lightly dust your surface with a little flour and roll out your cookie dough.
8. Use cookie cutters to cut shapes or hand roll balls and flatten them.
9. Place on your baking sheet. Bake for 12-16 minutes or until the edges look crisp and the center still a little soft.

Yummy to my Tummy!

Salted Caramel Brownie

1 ½ cups all purpose flour
4 eggs
3 cups granulated sugar
1 tsp salt
1tbsp vanilla extract
½ cup oil
1 cup unsweetened cocoa powder
¼ tsp baking powder
½ cup of semi sweet chocolate chips
1 cup of milk

1. Preheat oven to 350 degree F.
2. Grease a 13x9 inch baking pan.
3. In a bowl, combine all dry ingredients except chocolate chips.
4. In another bowl mix, whisk all wet ingredients except milk.
5. Slowly combine the two by alternating the dry ingredients with the milk. Once combined, fold in your chocolate chips.
6. Pour batter into baking pan and spread evenly.
7. Bake for 35-40 minutes or until just done. But don't over bake. Set aside to cool.

Caramel Topping

15 unwrapped caramel candies
2 tbsp heavy cream or half and half
Flaky sea salt

1. Place unwrapped caramels and heavy cream in a microwavable bowl and heat at 20-30 second increments. Stir occasionally until completely melted and smooth.
2. Pour the caramel sauce evenly over the brownies and sprinkle sea salt on top.
3. Cut when completely cooled.

Bon Appétit!

Smores Cookie Storyline

I don't know where Kyla discovered Smores but I'm guessing it would be YouTube. Kyla loves YouTube! She would watch educational shows over and over again. Then she would find the same show in multiple languages, and watch them as well. We are convinced that she has taught herself different languages. I'm quite sure her love for Smores is centered around the fact that she loves chocolate! She became so fond of them that she began to request them for breakfast. She now has a tabletop Smores maker that she enjoys. During the summer we take it outside for her to use. We want to avoid her learning to make them in the fire pit, so the Smores maker was a safer alternative. Sometimes you have to be creative so your child(ren) can enjoy the simple things in life.

Smores Cookies

1 pinch of salt
2 sticks of butter
2 eggs
¾ cup granulated sugar
¾ cup of brown sugar
2 tsp vanilla extract
1 ½ tsp baking soda
2 tsp cornstarch
2 cups semi sweet chocolate chips
2 cups mini marshmallows
2 ⅓ all purpose flour
1 cup crushed graham crackers

1. Preheat the oven to 375 degrees. Line a cookie sheet with parchment paper.
2. Cream together butter and sugars until light and fluffy.
3. Add eggs one at a time along with vanilla until combined.
4. In a separate bowl, combine flour, graham crackers crumbs, salt, baking soda and cornstarch. Whisk together.
5. Then slowly add the dry ingredients to the wet ingredients, making sure to occasionally scrape down the sides of your bowl.
6. Stir in chocolate chips and marshmallows.
7. Form balls of dough into 1 ½ inch balls and place on a sheet 1 ½ inches apart.
8. Bake at 375 degrees for 10 minutes. Allow cookies to cool on the sheet for 10 minutes.

And enjoy!

Spice Cake

2 ½ cups all purpose flour
2 teaspoons baking powder
1 teaspoon baking soda
½ teaspoon ground clove
2 teaspoons pumpkin pie spice
1 ⅓ cup of vegetable oil
1 ¾ cup of packed brown sugar
1 cup of unsweetened applesauce
4 eggs
2 teaspoons of vanilla extract

1. Preheat oven to 350 degrees F.
2. Whisk together all dry ingredients: flour, baking soda, baking powder, salt, cinnamon, and spices in a bowl.
3. In a separate bowl, whisk the oil, brown sugar, applesauce, eggs, and vanilla extract.
4. Pour the bowl of wet ingredients into the dry ingredients.
5. Pour combined mixture into your greased pan or pans, depending on the pan you are using.
6. Bake for 40 to 50 minutes or until a toothpick inserted into the center comes out clean.

Yummy!

Spice Muffin

2 cups all purpose flour
1 tsp baking soda
1tsp cinnamon
½ all spice
1 ⅓ cups granulated sugar
1 tsp vanilla extract
1 egg
½ cup unsalted butter
1 cup buttermilk

1. Preheat the oven to 350 degrees F.
2. Line your muffin tin with liners.
3. Using a stand or hand mixer, cream together 1 cup of the sugar, vanilla, and butter. Add your egg. Mix well.
4. Next, add your milk, flour, all spice, and baking soda. Mix well, but don't over mix.
5. Next, combine your remaining cup of sugar and cinnamon in a bowl and whisk together.
6. Add batter to the tins filling them halfway. Sprinkle some of the cinnamon/sugar mixture on top. Then fill the tins until almost filled. Sprinkle remaining cinnamon/sugar mixture evenly across the top of the muffins.
7. Use a toothpick to lightly swirl the batter in each tin.
8. Bake for 20-25 minutes or until an inserted toothpick comes out clean.
9. Cool in the pan for a few minutes then remove and place on the cooling rack.

Enjoy with your favorite ice cream!

Strawberry Buns

3 ¼ cups all purpose flour
1 pack instant active dry yeast
¼ cup sugar
1 egg
¾ cup milk
¼ cup water
½ tsp salt
⅓ cup butter

Filling

1 cup straw jam
½ tsp cinnamon
2 cups sliced strawberries

1. Preheat oven to 375 degree F.
2. Heat butter and milk together in a saucepan until warm and melted. Do not boil. Let cool until lukewarm.
3. In a large bowl, mix 2 ¼ cups of flour with all of your other dry ingredients. Mix well.
4. Now stir in egg and water and mix well.
5. Stir in the milk mixture until dough forms. Make sure your milk is lukewarm. You will need the warmth to activate the yeast in the dough.
6. Add remaining flour to the dough and form a nice ball. Using floured hands, place dough on a floured surface and knead until smooth. Return dough to the bowl, cover with a damp towel and let rest for 10 minutes.
7. Roll dough into a 15x10 inch rectangular shape. Spread the jam all over it. Sprinkle it with cinnamon. Spread your strawberries evenly across the surface of the dough.
8. Roll the dough into a log and pinch the seams. Cut the log into 12 equal sized rolls. Place rolls cut side up, side by side in a greased 11x13 inch baking pan.
9. Cover with a damp cloth and let rise for 30 minutes.
10. Bake in the oven for 30 minutes or until golden brown. Once cooled, spread or pour glaze over rolls (glaze recipe included in this book).

Yummy to my tummy!

Strawberry Cake

2 ¾ cups all purpose flour
4 eggs
1 cup of butter
1 ¾ cups granulated sugar
1 3.4oz box of instant strawberry pudding
2 ½ tsp baking powder
1 cup of whole milk
1 tbsp vanilla extract
1 tbsp strawberry extract
1 cup pureed fresh strawberries
½ tsp salt

1. Preheat oven to 350 degree F.
2. Grease and flour (or spray with cooking spray) two 8 inch baking pans.
3. Simmer your strawberry puree on the stove until it is reduced to a ½ cup. Set aside and let it completely cool.
4. In a large bowl, mix all of your dry ingredients, including the pudding mix.
5. In another bowl, using a stand or hand mixer, cream together your butter and sugar until fluffy.
6. Next, add and your eggs one at a time and mix well. Then add your vanilla and strawberry extracts.
7. Once combined, begin adding your flour mixture to the butter mixture. Alternating with the milk.
8. Beat well after each addition to the batter. Once combined, fold in your pureed strawberries.
9. Pour batter evenly into your baking pans and bake from 30-40 minutes or until an inserted toothpick comes out clean.
10. Cool for 10 minutes in the pan. Then finish cooling on a rack.

Bon Appétit!

Vanilla Cake

2 ½ cups all purpose flour
1 3.4 oz pack of instant vanilla pudding
1 ½ tbsp vanilla extract
1 ½ half cups granulated sugar
2 ½ tbsp baking powder
1 ¼ cup whole milk
¼ tsp salt
6 oz. unsalted butter
⅓ cup sourcream
3 eggs

1. Preheat the oven to 350 degree F.
2. Grease and flour (or spray with cooking spray) two 8-inch baking pans. Set aside.
3. In a bowl, mix all dry ingredients together.
4. Using a stand or hand mixer, cream together your sugar and butter until light and fluffy.
5. Next, add your eggs one at a time until incorporated. And your vanilla.
6. Begin mixing in the dry ingredients, alternating with the milk.
7. Sour cream will be your last wet ingredient. Add that now.
8. Then add the last of your flour mixture, your final ingredient. Mix on high for 10 seconds.
9. Evenly divide the batter into your cake pans and bake for 40 minutes to 1 hour. Or until a toothpick comes out clean.
10. Cool in pans for 10 minutes. Then place on racks to complete cooling.

Yum!

Vanilla Cupcake Storyline

My baking business started with cupcakes and Kyla. Before Kyla was diagnosed with Autism, we could not understand her behavior patterns. She wouldn't sleep at night or sit still when awake. We often awaken and found that she pulled all of her clothing out of the dresser drawers and on to the floor. We were lost as to what was happening. I have always loved cooking and baking. So the house is filled with cookbooks. One day Kyla discovered one of my baking cookbooks and we realized it kept her still. She was mesmerized by the bright pictures. From that point on, we bought every baking cookbook we could find, especially the ones filled with bright illustrations! Kyla's favorite cookbook was a cupcake book. So when I decided to start a baking business, Cupcakes was my focus.

Vanilla Confetti Cupcakes

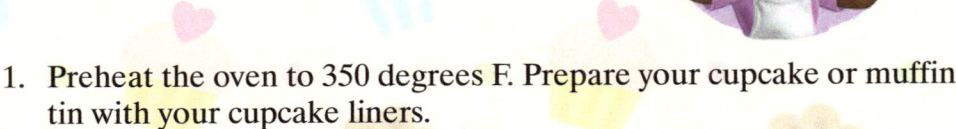

2 ¾ cups all purpose flour
1 ½ cups granulated sugar
2 tsp baking powder
¾ tsp baking soda
⅝ tsb salt
2 tbsp vanilla extract
4 eggs
½ cup vegetable oil
1 ¾ cups unsalted butter
1 cup buttermilk

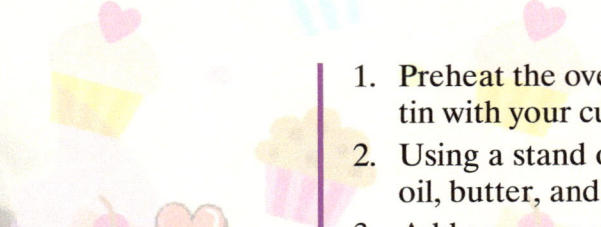

1. Preheat the oven to 350 degrees F. Prepare your cupcake or muffin tin with your cupcake liners.
2. Using a stand or hand mixer and bowl, beat on medium speed the oil, butter, and sugar together until light and fluffy.
3. Add eggs one at a time, until mixed well. Then add vanilla.
4. Next, in a separate bowl, combine all of the dry ingredients. Whisk together.
5. Add half of the dry ingredients to the wet mixer and mix on low speed until almost combined.
6. At this point, pour in your buttermilk and the remaining dry ingredients. Mix on low until just combined. Do not over mix.
7. Scoop your batter into your baking tins. Bake for 12-15 minutes or until an inserted toothpick comes out clean.

Let cool, frost, and enjoy.

White chocolate chip cookies

3 cups all purpose flour
1 cup of granulated sugar
1 cup of packed brown sugar
1 teaspoon of baking soda
½ teaspoon of salt
2 cups semi-sweet white chocolate chips
2 eggs
2 teaspoon of hot water
2 teaspoon of vanilla extract
1 cup of soften unsalted butter

1. Preheat oven 300 degrees F.
2. Cream together your butter, white sugar, and brown sugar until smooth.
3. Beat in your eggs one at a time. Then stir in your vanilla.
4. Dissolve baking soda in the hot water. Add the mixture and salt to your creamed mixture.
5. Then stir in the flour and white chocolate chips.
6. Drop large spoonfuls on to an ungreased cookie sheet.
7. Bake 10-13 minutes, depending on the size of your drops.

Bon Appétit!

Meet Kyla

Kyla is a fun loving kid with a bubble personality. Unlike some Autistic children, she has always loved hugs and nose kisses. She loves baking and eating. Her favorites are seafood and sunflower seeds. And she loves swings and jumping in the jumpy. What makes her happiest is family gatherings. She LOVES to be around family.

If you have a child with special needs, we encourage you to find things that make them happy, and participate in the activities with them. This cookbook can be a start of a beautiful and fun memory maker! Take lots of pictures, make a mess in the kitchen, and enjoy the history-making experience to treasure for the rest of your life. No go and have fun baking!

www.ingramcontent.com/pod-product-compliance
Lightning Source LLC
Chambersburg PA
CBHW041953150426
43199CB00004B/28